GOOD FOOD

Grains

Julia Adams

PowerKiDS
press.
New York

Published in 2011 by The Rosen Publishing Group Inc.
29 East 21st Street, New York, NY 10010

First Edition

Editor: Julia Adams
Managing Editor: Victoria Brooker
Designer: Paul Cherrill
Picture Researcher: Julia Adams
Food and Nutrition Consultant: Ester Davies
Photo Models: Asha Francis, Lydia Washbourne

Library of Congress Cataloguing-in-Publication Data

Adams, Julia, 1979-
Grains / by Julia Adams. -- 1st ed.
    p. cm. -- (Good food)
Includes index.
ISBN 978-1-4488-3273-6 (library binding)
1. Grain--Juvenile literature. I. Title. II. Series: Adams, Julia,
1979- Good food.
SB189.A43 2011
633.1--dc22

                                2010023707

Photographs:
Andy Crawford: 21, 22, 23; Getty: Dorling Kindersley 19;
iStock: Grafissimo 4, nicolesy 5, dlerick 16; Shutterstock:
juliengrondin 1/14, Pinkcandy 2/13, Suzanne Tucker OFC/6,
Gorilla 7, Elena Elisseeva 8, Kodda 9, Terrance Emerson 10,
Thomas M Perkins 11, OlegD 12, Denis and Yulia Pogostins
13, Yuri Arcurs 15, Sadeugra 17, Monkey Business Images 18,
Kristiana007 20.

Manufactured in China
CPSIA Compliance Information: Batch #WAW1102PK: For Further Information
contact Rosen Publishing, New York, New York at 1-800-237-9932

Web Sites

Contents

Good for You

Everyone needs to eat the right kind of food to stay healthy. The food we eat comes from plants and animals.

Many of the foods we eat are made from grains. Grains come from plants.

Grains are good for us because they give us energy. They also have vitamins and minerals that help us to stay healthy.

Bread is made from grains such as wheat and rye.

What Are Grains?

Grains are grass plants, such as wheat, oats, and rice. They have a tall, thin stalk. At the top of the stalk, the plants grow seeds that are also called grains.

Can you see where the grains are growing on these oat plants?

We cook grains in many different ways. Sometimes we boil them. A lot of grains, such as wheat and rye, are crushed, or ground, to make flour.

We use flour to bake bread and cakes.

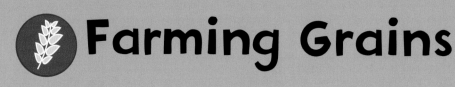 Farming Grains

Grain plants are grown on farms. The farmer plants them in huge fields. When the grain plants are ripe, they are harvested.

When grain plants start growing, they look just like grass. This is a field of wheat.

The grains are harvested by big machines called combine harvesters. Combine harvesters separate the grain from the rest of the plant.

This combine harvester is filling a tractor with wheat grains.

The little pockets that grains grow in are called husks.

9

Wheat

The most popular grain in the world is wheat. We use it to make many kinds of foods. It is often ground into flour in mills.

This is a mill. The tall towers are used to store flour.

We use wheat flour to make bread, pasta, pizza, pies, cakes, and cookies. It is used to make pancakes and to thicken sauces, too.

We make cookies using wheat flour.

 # Rye

Rye grains look very similar to wheat grains, but they are darker. Rye can be boiled and eaten instead of rice or in salads.

This is boiled rye. It has a slightly stronger taste than rice.

Rye is often ground into flour to make bread. Rye bread is very dense and darker than wheat bread.

wheat bread

rye bread

Can you see the difference between rye bread and wheat bread?

Rice

The fields that rice is grown in are called paddies. They are flooded with water. The ripe grains are either picked by hand or by machine.

This farmer is planting rice seedlings in a paddy.

You have to boil rice to eat it. Many dishes from around the world use rice. Sometimes, rice is popped by heating it at a high temperature.

We eat popped rice as a breakfast cereal.

Can you think of a dessert that is made of rice?

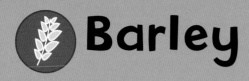

Barley

The grains of the barley plant are used to make both food and drinks. We boil barley and add it to soups and stews. It can be eaten like rice, too.

Can you see the white barley grains in this soup?

16

Barley is also soaked and dried
to make malt syrup. This is added to
food and drinks to make them sweet.

Juice drinks
are sometimes
sweetened with
malt syrup.

Oats

Oat grains are often steamed and then rolled into flakes. We eat rolled oats raw in muesli or cooked in oatmeal.

Oatmeal and fruit make a delicious and healthy breakfast.

Rolled oats are also used in baking.
Oat bars, cookies, and cobblers
are made with rolled oats.

Rolled oats were used to make
the top of this fruit cobbler.

Corn

Corn grows on cobs. Each cob has 16 rows of corn kernels. The dried corn kernels are used as grains.

Can you see the kernels on this corncob?

Corn kernels are often ground into flour to make bread. They are also rolled and baked to make cornflakes.

Corn kernels can be heated and popped to make popcorn.

Fresh corn is also eaten as a vegetable. Then we call it sweet corn.

Make Your Own Muesli

You Will Need:
- bowl · knife · rolled oats
- popped rice · cornflakes
- pumpkin seeds · sunflower seeds · dried apricots
- raisins · nuts

Follow the steps of this recipe to make some delicious muesli for your breakfast.

1. Add the rolled oats, the popped rice, and the cornflakes to the bowl and stir with a spoon.

2. Add the pumpkin seeds and the sunflower seeds to the mix. You can add sesame seeds and linseeds, too.

3. Take a handful of dried apricots. Ask an adult to help you cut each of them in half. Add them to the mix.

4. Add the raisins to the bowl. If you like nuts, you can add a handful of nuts as well.

5. To serve, add some fresh, cut fruit to your muesli and pour milk on it. You can also use yogurt or fruit juice.

6. Enjoy your delicious breakfast!

Glossary and Further Information

dense when something is tightly packed

harvest to pick a plant that is ripe

kernels the grains from a corn plant

mill a machine that grinds grains into flour

minerals substances in food that keep our bodies healthy. Calcium is a mineral that helps to build strong bones.

ripe when a plant is ready to eat

vitamins substances in food that help keep our bodies healthy and stop us from catching colds

Books

Healthy Eating: Grains
by Nancy Dickmann
(Heinemann Educational, 2010)

The Grain Group
by Mari Schuh
(Capstone Press, 2006)

Index